I0425751

100 Thoughts and Insights

OLAREWAJU OLADIPO

Copyright © 2019 Olarewaju Oladipo
All rights reserved. Published by Wundia Books.
Wundia and associated logos are trademarks and/or registered
trademarks.
Learn about the author @doctoroladipo on
Facebook/Twitter/Instagram/Pinterest/Google+, and on the
web - **www.olarewajuoladipo.com**

Cover design - Wundia Books.

No part of this publication may be published in whole or in part,
or stored in a retrieval system, or transmitted in any form or by
any means, electronic, mechanical, photocopying, recording, or
otherwise, without written permission of the publisher. For
information regarding permission, write to Wundia Books, PO
Box 446, Canton MA 02021 USA

First Printing, March 2019

FOREWORD

100 Thoughts and Insights is a collection of personal observations that explore the complexities of life and examine the age-old wisdom of living. This book is the second of a collection of literary works that first originated from daily reflections in my personal journey through life.

I sincerely hope that in reading this book, you will find aspects of it that you can apply in your pursuit of a life full of peace and joy.

ACKNOWLEDGEMENT

This book is dedicated to all those who continue to support our work at 3SqMeals.

The best gift I can ever receive is a gift I can always use, one that is best enjoyed when shared with others, a gift that doubles with every person I share it with. The best gift I can ever give is a gift I never buy, one that comes back to me, a gift that all of us can give - Love.

Your thought is a unique key.
In your thought is your voice;
in your thought is your dream;
in your thought is your drive;
in your thought is your health;
in your thought is your wealth;
in your thought is your joy;
in your thought is your peace;
in your thought is your strength.

If you have never known anything but great success, do not take it as your birthright. If you have never known anything but dismal failure, do not take it as your destiny. No one deliberately courts failure, but many will never attain success without a prior encounter with failure.

If you say there is no way, it is because you do not know any better. If you say there is no way, it is because you do not see any better. If you say there is no way, it is because you do not think any better. If you say there is no way, it is because you do not dream any better.

Through your words, your heart speaks; through your actions, your heart beats; through your attitude, your heart flows; through your smile, your heart feels; through your kindness, your heart gives; through your forgiveness, your heart lives; through your love, your heart shines.

In your search for a big miracle, do not forget to be thankful for the small victories that the day brings and to celebrate the lesser miracles that life gifts to you, for the seeds of many miracles are sowed when we express sincere appreciation for the small miracles in our lives.

Your shadow is the closest image of self, a reflection for others to praise or condemn, an image that manifests once you are illuminated, an image that changes with your relationship to the truth, an image that stays hidden if you elect to stay in darkness. You are not invisible.

In doing lies who you are. I am not a dancer, but I dance. I am not a swimmer, but I swim. I am not an athlete, but I sprint. I am not an artist, but I paint. I am not an author, but I write. I am not a speaker, but I speak. I am not a teacher, but I teach. In doing lies who you are.

For every quiet voice that prompts you to relentlessly pursue your desire, there is a quieter voice that challenges your motivation. Self-doubt is a friendly enemy, an undesirable voice that you have to silence at all times, and with all your being, to pursue all that you desire.

Without my mind, my mouth is only a mouth; without my mind, my hand is only a hand; without my mind, my eye is only an eye; without my mind, my ear is only an ear; without my mind, my head is only a head; without my mind, my nose is only a nose; without my mind, I am only a body.

The path to gain through pain is not for the faint-hearted. The path to gain through pain is not for the feeble-minded. The path to gain through pain is not for the heavy-footed. The path to gain through pain is not for the wrong-headed. Never wait for the pain-free pass to gain.

Truth has no attribute - it has no color, no taste, no texture, and no smell. Truth has no boundary - it has no heritage, no tribe, no race, and no citizen. Truth has no language - it has no dialect, no accent, and no translation. Truth has no feature - it has no hands and no feet.

To prepare is to excel, but never view preparation as a substitute for your real act. In taking your first bold steps, you sow the seeds of excellence, turn imperfection into an asset, and make fear a tool for survival. No amount of rehearsal can replace the experience of a real act.

Change is pervasive, even among the most resistant of spirits; change is universal, even among the most marginal of humans; change is dear, even among the most welcoming of souls; change is unsettling, even among the most settled of minds. Change is what we ignore in the obvious.

There is one thing we all can do better - nothing big, nothing extraordinary, nothing demanding of ourselves. There is one thing we all can do better, something we used to do, something we still do, something we all still take for granted. We can never care enough for one another.

Many beginnings go unnoticed, lack funfair, and mean little, until they form seeds of greatness. Many beginnings look ordinary, seem nominal, and bear little, until they birth fruits of wonder. Many beginnings feel lonely, take time, and say little, until they form roots of legacy.

Never wait for success to feel successful; never wait for happiness to feel happy; never wait for accomplishment to feel accomplished; never wait for hope to feel hopeful; never wait for recognition to feel recognized. To be all you want to be is to behave the way you want to be.

Deception is man's way of fooling with human perception. Silence is man's way of messing with human emotion. Denial is man's way of playing with human existence. Vanity is man's way of experimenting with human sanity. Condescension is man's way of interfering with human civility.

The two poles of an expedition, its start and its finish, tell a little about the experiences of those who made the journey. To allow yourself to be defined by your beginning is to refuse to begin at all; to allow yourself to be defined by your destination is to give up trying.

To rejoice at the humiliation of others is to display ignorance of the frailty of human morality. To marvel at the shortcomings of others is to display naiveté of the fallibility of mankind. To pride in one's holiness is to display irreverence for the virtue of grace to mankind.

You don't have to search for your personal gift as if it is a lost item of jewelry; you don't have to search for your life's purpose as if it is a lost piece of art. Your purpose will find you if you help others find theirs; your gift will find you if you help others find theirs.

The temporal dimension to understanding dictates that the wise words of a sage are never fully deciphered by the untamed ears of the unseasoned. To bridge the gap of understanding is to navigate the shadow of the valley of ignorance and seek the wisdom of those advanced in years.

A dream is a feat when achieved, a victory when conquered, a triumph when overcome, a miracle when fulfilled, an adventure when experienced, a delight when shared, a pride when accomplished, a conquest when earned, a joy when witnessed, but a pure desire when only imagined.

Visualize six imaginary lines originating from you and beaming upward, downward, sideways, forward, and backward. See the many paths in which life can take you that inhabit the earth. As there are many ways that life can set your course, so are the ways we are endowed to navigate through life.

Reciprocity breeds insincerity — we like others in the hope that we will be liked. Reciprocity breeds contempt — we follow others in the hope that we will be followed. Reciprocity breeds disappointment — we befriend others in the hope that we will be befriended. Expect no return.

For every friend that you make, be thankful; for every adversary that you identify, be joyful. For every well-wisher that you meet, be hopeful; for every foe that you encounter, be patient. For every supporter that you win, be grateful; for every hater that you see, be prayerful.

The ultimate in the practice of enlightened self-interest is in the act of unconditional forgiveness, for everyone who is motivated enough to unreservedly let go of whoever wronged them stands to benefit immensely from the gesture, far more than the person they choose to forgive.

In thanksgiving, I see my past in its meaning; in thanksgiving, I see my present in its purity; in thanksgiving, I see my future in its glory. Thanksgiving is for all time— in the good and the not-so-good times. A life lived with thanksgiving is a life destined for fulfillment.

To truly become is to make others become. To get a miracle, work miracles in others. To live in harmony, breed harmony in others. To achieve real happiness, create happiness for others. To imagine your future, imagine a future with others. To truly become is to make others become.

To change your circumstance, you have to know exactly what you want; to blame your circumstance, you have to know exactly what you don't want. An awareness of your circumstance is of no value if you choose to do nothing with the knowledge and refuse to change your circumstance.

The most difficult questions to ask
are those that we ask ourselves, for
in such questions lie the solutions
to our struggles. The most difficult
answers to give are those that we
already know, for in such answers
lie the solutions to our struggles.
Dare to answer your questions.

There is a light that shines from every human, one that is visible to others but may not be visible to you, a light that is a reflection of who you really are, one that can only be concealed for so long and, once revealed, tells the whole world the kind of person you really are.

The beauty of the past lies in the opportunities it grant us to view it as we please; the beauty of the present lies in the opportunities it grant us to live with it as we please; the beauty of the future lies in the opportunities it grant us to imagine it as we please.

Assume every new day is the beginning of your life. Look for one thing that you could do today to make your life better tomorrow. Look for one person, and do one thing today for them to make their life better tomorrow. Every new day is an opportunity of a new beginning.

Your enemy has a lot in common with your friend — they teach you the lessons of life. Your enemy has a lot in common with your friend — they can switch their allegiance. Your enemy has a lot in common with your friend — they can shape your destiny. Treat your enemy like a friend.

The more air of wisdom you breathe, the more you will see. The more water of wisdom you drink, the more you will thirst. The more fragrance of wisdom you sprinkle, the more you will perceive. The more seeds of wisdom you plant, the more you will prosper.

Oddities of life: a chipped tooth, a misplaced key, a paper cut, a high bill, a spilled drink, a flat tire, a parking ticket, a missed flight, a cancelled date, a late fee, a lost mail, a stolen package, a broken nail, a dead phone, a bad meal, a voided coupon. Oddities of life.

What man calls discovery, the heaven calls revelation; what man calls success, the heaven calls victory; what man calls wisdom, the heaven calls enlightenment; what man calls chance, the heaven calls grace; what man calls dream, the heaven calls destiny. Let heaven speak for you.

The wisdom of one at a time says know thy limit. You can only see through one pair of lenses at a time. You can only drink from a cup of water at a time. You can only walk in one pair of shoes at a time. You can only race in one direction at a time. You can only think one thought a time.

Time is one special gift that is bestowed upon every person that morning wakes up on this planet. It is one gift that you must use in its entirety before the day runs out. You have an obligation to this planet to do the most possible in good deeds before the day runs out.

Knowledge is as good as ignorance
if the one in possession of
knowledge does not recognize it.
Knowledge is as good as ignorance
if the one in possession of
knowledge does not respect it.
Knowledge is as good as ignorance
if the one in possession of
knowledge does not utilize it.

In you, your circumstance and your surrounding are the tools that you will need for survival. Without you, the instinct for survival does not exist. Without your circumstance, there is nothing to fight for. Without your surroundings, what you need for survival seems out of reach.

The person who asks for help and receives 'no' for an answer and the person who assumes 'no' for an answer and refuses to ask for help see rejection through different sets of eyes. The worst form of rejection is one which, due to irrational fear, we elect to impose upon ourselves.

There are three gated entrances to the roads that lead to opportunities: one entrance has its gate fully closed, the second has its gate wide open, but the third has its gate open yet shielded with an impenetrable curtain. A guarded, open door is no different from a closed door.

The greatest thief of all times is never out to pilfer your jewelry, art collections, or your luxury goods but is always in search of that piece of you that matters most to any human: your mind. However, your mind is one piece of you that you can lose without realizing it's gone. Beware!

There is a gift that stands the test of time, one that you can never give or get enough of; a gift that has no unit of measure, costs so little, but yields in multiple folds; a gift that many yearn for, but few dare to ask for, a gift for the young and the old - the gift of encouragement.

To guard your senses is to guard your mind. What you hear has the potential to shape your thoughts. What you see has the power to change your heart. What you feel has the strength to define your actions. What you witness has the influence to mold your conscience. Guard your senses.

A change of habit is the closest many will experience to the battle of change, a transformative process that never happens unless you harness the power of sheer determination and divine intervention. Lasting change only happens when true desire aligns with ethereal force. You are not alone.

The language of a smile is as varied as the faces that fill the planet. The meaning of a smile is as unique as the humans that tread the earth. There is no human gesture as complex as that which the face reveals: the real emotion that lies beneath the smile on the face of a stranger.

A dream, though pure at birth, is prone to contamination by doubt and subject to the forces of apathy. A dream, though original at birth, is liable to the effect of inertia and open to the wind of stupor. A dream is only a dream until the dreamer takes hold of their destiny.

The best kept secrets in life are not always those secured in the safest of vaults or those buried in the most secretive of minds, but they are those left in the open for all to see yet remain unrecognized by all who walk by it and lack the understanding and the wisdom to see the obvious.

Time is not yours until you claim it.
Time is not yours until you plan it.
Time is not yours until you use it.
Time is not yours until you hold it.
Time is not yours until you gift it.
Time is not yours until you receive
it. Time is not yours until you time
it. Time is not instantly yours.

No one has it all. The poorest among us has a gem that the richest among us wish they had; the weakest among us has a strength that the strongest among us wish they possessed; the least famous among us has a freedom that the most famous among us wish they enjoyed. No one has it all.

The best of humanity is in our hands. The best of humanity is only possible when our hands unfold to hold another person's hands, our shoulders are positioned to offer someone else a lift, and our feet are planted to clear a path for another person. The best of humanity is in our hands.

Whenever two or more people gather together in harmony, there is the potential for disharmony from within. The fruit of discord is always low-lying and within the reach of anyone that is unwilling to make the investment needed to cultivate a united front. Real peace is not free.

The deep thoughts of the heart of man is an enigma — one that no locksmith can open, no algorithm can predict, no codebreaker can decipher, no surgeon can dissect, no jailer can imprison, no astrologist can read, no explorer can map, and no artist can draw. So is the heart of man.

To master time is to master your destiny. To mine time is to secure your destiny. To respect time is to nurture your destiny. To free time is to free your destiny. To give time is to share your destiny. To waste time is to defer your destiny. Without time, destiny has no meaning.

The past is often a source of distraction for the living. Without it, the present has no history to rely on; with it, the future has a history to work with. The weight you give to your future is your prerogative— it is the greatest power you have to right the wrong in your past.

Every single day, some people will suddenly wake up to see the beauty in what was once abandoned. Every single day, some people will suddenly wake up to see the treasure in what was once ignored. To wake up to true reality, even though it may be sudden, is not always intentional.

For everything that you possess and take for granted, there are many people that would give their worlds to have the grace that comes with it. For everything that you lack and so covet, there are many people that would give their worlds to part with the burden that comes with it.

What money can buy is often limited by the unit of measurement for the material being exchanged. The things that money cannot buy often lack a unit of measurement, but they define the ideals that both the wealthy and the impoverished constantly aspire to achieve.

Fear and worry make a toxic cocktail that never fails to harm whoever elects to sip from its cup, a mix that is bound to tear apart whoever knowingly drinks from its cup. Rather than succumb to the temptation, strive to let the cup pass whenever life serves you a potion of strife.

The person who has one minute at their disposal and the person who has twenty-four hours at their disposal often give the same reason— being busy—for failing to make the most of what life has to offer. Being busy is our worldly excuse for letting our 'heaven on earth' slip by.

In your seventies, you cherish the years. In your sixties, you feel the years. In your fifties, you think the years. In your forties, you work the years. In your thirties, you count the years. In your twenties, you see the years. At every age, live like you are in your seventies.

If you are left with just one conversation to have on this planet, make it one that happens between you and your soul, for every human's journey on earth is powered by a force that resides deep within their soul, without which our existence on earth would be physical and ordinary.

If a negative personal experience does not motivate you to do good, a positive one may never alter your mind. It is better to make joy your motivation to do good than to wait for your world to be turned upside down to show empathy towards others. To do good, no experience is needed.

It is quite possible to claim another person's prophecy as your own; it is quite possible to adopt another person's destiny as your own. You have no part to play in what is prophesied over your life, but you are somehow responsible for how you let a prophecy dominate your destiny.

To be different, you really don't have to try hard, for what you need to be different is not on the outside but within you. Your difference is not what defines your individuality, but the difference you make in the lives of those whose paths cross yours is paramount to your being.

You never have a say on your
choice of enemies—those within
ourselves and those from the
outside. The enemy within is not
always subject to your control and
takes the whole of you to conquer.
The enemy from the outside is
often subject to your control, but it
takes a bit of you.

In a two-way conversation, you have more than two voices at work, for what we say is often not what is heard by the other party. In a two-way conversation, you need more than four ears at work, for what we hear is often not what is said by the other party. No reality is absolute.

A genuine blessing is a reward for a service you hardly offered, a gift of a material you barely deserve, a privilege of a status you cannot justify, an accolade for a milestone you never attained, a luxury of a life you least imagined, and a legacy of a destiny you can't believe.

On the road to success, acknowledge those who elect to encourage, many who offer to assist, and all whose counsel are instrumental in getting you to your final destination. Do the same to those who set obstacles in your path, for without them you may have never found your success.

To imagine the experience of others is to see through their eyes. To encounter the experience of others is to see through your eyes. You may never experience all there is to experience in this beautiful world, but through the eyes of others you can use your power of imagination.

Your ears are most accustomed to hearing your voice. Your eyes are most adapted to seeing your vision. Your nose is most sensitive to odors other than yours. Your feet are seasoned to walk on familiar paths. Your mind is trained to express your thought. No one person knows it all.

In the pursuit of your dream, remember that undesirable diversions may herald an impending serendipity; do not allow your preoccupation with the moment to rob you of the promise of a greater future, and never believe the fallacy that an uncharted course is a sure recipe for failure.

No traveler begins a journey without the final destination in their hearts. No traveler begins a journey without the path to the final destination in their hearts. The journey of life is never fully defined by its beginning, its path, or its destination, but by a sum of its parts.

To be born with a gift is not the same as having a talent. Out of the word 'talent' is the word 'latent', a word that defines what becomes of many unnurtured gifts. Until you encounter those who see in you the gifts you never thought you had, you may never discover your talents.

A minute can be really long; a minute can be really short. Those with abundance of time know not the luxury they have in their possession; those with a dearth of time know well the reality of poverty of time. Time is not yours until you exploit it—intentionally or accidentally.

A ray of enlightenment is all it takes to uncover a lifetime of folly. A flash of awareness is all it takes to unravel the bliss of ignorance. A spark of revelation is all it takes to transform the halo of confusion. A glitter of hope is all it takes to destroy the fog of despair.

The nights that precede an overnight success are many. The zeros that begin a heroic performance are numerous. The breaks that herald a breakthrough are countless. The miles that lead to a milestone are endless. The steps that culminate in a victory lap are painful. No giving up.

There are no ordinary people, but there are people who see themselves as ordinary. There are no ordinary teams, but there are teams who see themselves as ordinary. What you believe will become your vision; what you perceive will become your reality. See the extraordinary in you.

Self-doubt you can tame, for it is within. Self-esteem you can fix for it is within. Self-confidence you can build, for it is within. Self-awareness you can grow, for it is within. Self-fulfillment you can achieve, for it is within. To obsess with the self is to be enslaved by your ego.

Your smile is the greatest art you will ever make. Your smile is the finest make-up you will ever wear. Your smile is the brightest light you will ever shine. Your smile is the warmest embrace you can ever give. Your smile is the best impression you can ever give. Own your smile.

There is no best time for a good decision, but every good decision turns out to be timely. There is no best time to change for good, but every change for good turns out to be timely. There is no best time to pursue your dream, but every big dream turns out to be timely.

It's time.

To have the freedom to choose is to have a choice. To have a choice is to discover your options. To discover your options is to know your field. To know your field is to open your eyes. To open your eyes is to see beyond the obvious. To see beyond the obvious is to be free indeed.

To shape your destiny, you need a
compass. To prove your destiny,
you need a vision. To live your
destiny, you need a dream. To walk
your destiny, you need a path. To
see your destiny, you need a light.
To claim your destiny, you need a
ticket. No one's destiny is fixed by
birth.

Your mind is the greatest asset you will ever own; your thought is the strongest weapon you will ever have; your dream is the biggest fantasy you will ever live; your walk is the longest journey you will ever make; your hope is the brightest promise you will ever keep. All yours.

Happiness is not only the most feigned of all emotions, it is the most difficult of all emotions to decipher in its sincerest form. An outward display of happiness is sometimes a camouflage for melancholy shrouded in a mask of falsehood. To fake happiness is the extreme of deceit.

Doing the same thing every day for a guaranteed outcome is the routine for all those who cherish certainty over the not-so-secure alternatives. What you achieve from your aversion to an insecure future is sometimes lost in the agony of the unfulfilled promises that shape your destiny.

In the playground of life, ride the rollercoaster with care, embrace the trampoline with caution, pursue the trail with vigilance, travel the course with boldness, handle the swing with respect, and swim the course with tenacity. The playground of life is not just all about play.

Time is what it takes to succeed while timing is what takes you to success. To succeed, you may have the authority to mine time, but no human has the authority to time success. In your walk through the path of success, pray that what you fail to do with time is granted to you in time.

To be different, you don't have to try. To stand out, you don't have to shout. To be known, you don't have to talk. To look strong, you don't have to fight. To take pride, you don't have to boast. To take lead, you don't have to wait. To feel good, you don't have to ask. Be you.

To despair is to miss the spark of light in the middle of darkness, to ignore the droplet of water in the heart of the desert, and to fail to breathe through a lifeline of air in the depth of an ocean. Hope is for the living. To give up is to allow desperation to take hold of you.

The fear of what will be is no different from the fear of what will not be to all those who willingly submit to its torment. To live in constant fear is to live in constant misery. Morbid fear has a singularity of purpose: to steal your soul while you are still living. Fear not.

It is one thing to give; it is another thing to give cheerfully. It is one thing to give cheerfully; it is another thing to meet the need of the receiver. Every act of giving must be done with the humility of heart and a simple prayer that we meet the receiver where their need is.

To learn, you must be aware of other people's past mistakes. To thrive, you must be aware of your past mistakes. To excel, you must avoid repeating other people's past mistakes. To prosper, you must avoid making the same mistake twice. Never judge people solely by their mistakes.

Never worry about finding your purpose, but worry about how to treat your fellow human beings. Never worry about your fulfillment, but worry about how to fill up the spirit of those empty. Purpose is meaningless if it is all about you. Fulfillment is vanity if it is self-serving.

In doing good, remember one out of three persons will never pay you back nor pay it forward, one out of three persons will cause you to question if your sacrifice was worth it, and one out of three persons will pay you back in the same token or pay it forward in multiple folds.

To know a friend, you have to test a friend; to know a foe, you have to test a foe. A foe will masquerade as a friend to ride the boat of friendship until the tides of life turn. A friend will be mistaken for a foe as you maneuver through life's troubled waters. Know thy enemies.

The most informed any human can be is to have a real sense of what is not known—the known unknown. There is no worse form of ignorance than one that exists without any sense of self awareness. The conscious pursuit of the extent of one's ignorance is the beginning of knowledge.

For every sacrifice that a human makes, there is every possibility that it may result in absolutely nothing. The determination to apply your best in the pursuit of what is deemed impossible can only come from within you. Never trust another human for what is impossible.

ABOUT THE AUTHOR

Olarewaju Oladipo is an author (fiction and non-fiction) whose writing career began while practicing as an orthopedic surgeon. Following the release of his earlier books "The White Coat" (2006) and "House Calls" (2007), he dedicated the next few years to crafting motivational quotes written using the Twitter handle @3SqMeals as Dr. O' and publishing multiple books under the '3SqMeals Tweets – Not Your Typical Meal' series.

His works of fiction include the "North Main Street" mystery series and the "Once A Doc" medical fiction series, with the release of Barber's Haven (2015), 'A Patient called Emma' (2015) and 'Ghost Bus (2016).

'The Sculpture Garden' series is based on actual sculptures and part of an ongoing effort to support the work of local artists in Nigeria, fund the establishment of sustainable sculpture gardens, and sponsor worldwide collaborations with art institutions.

Two Blind Men (2017) was the first of a collection of short stories of the 'Sculpture Garden' series. Tortoise of Many Colors (2017), The Tree of Wonder (2017), and Esther (2018) are other books in the series.

100 Prayers and Whispers (2018) is the first book in a series devoted to daily reflections of the author as shared using a dedicated Twitter handle - @3SqMeals.

All books are available in paperbacks and eBook formats on Amazon, Kobo, Smashwords, and on author's website (www.olarewajuoladipo.com).

www.ingramcontent.com/pod-product-compliance
Lightning Source LLC
Chambersburg PA
CBHW051355280526
45784CB00007B/2965